A Story of Saint John Bosco

A Story of Saint John Bosco

By
Brother Ernest, C.S.C.

Pictures by
Carolyn Lee Jagodits

Neumann Press
Charlotte, North Carolina

Nihil Obstat:
C. F. Brooks, C.S.C.
Censor Deputatus

Cum Permissu:
Brother Donatus Schmitz, C.S.C
Provincial

Imprimatur:
✝ Most Rev. Leo A. Pursley, D.D.
Bishop of Fort Wayne-South Bend

A Story of St. John Bosco

ISBN 978-0-911845-04-4

Printed and bound in the United States of America.

Neumann Press
Charlotte, North Carolina
www.NeumannPress.com

2013

Dedication
To Brother Liborius, C. S. C.

A STORY OF SAINT JOHN BOSCO

Little Johnny Bosco came into this world on August 16, 1815. He was born in a town in Italy known as Becchi. He was quite like any other little fellow—except that when he got to be about ten years old he liked to study better than to play. But there are a lot of lads like that.

And the reason why John liked to study was because he thought he wanted to be a priest some day.

John's mother was a good lady. She often told him about God and Our Lady. It helped him to be good.

One day John went with his father to a fair. There he saw a man doing wonderful tricks. John watched him carefully. Then, when he got home, John tried to do them. He began by tossing saucers into the air, trying to keep three of them in motion at once. And he did it, too! From that day young Bosco learned many tricks. Soon he became the best entertainer in the whole village.

Then what do you think John did?

Well, there were a lot of boys in the village. Some of them were pretty rough. Most of them didn't know much about their religion. John got them to come to his father's barn. There he had a platform built. When all were together, John did some of his best tricks. The boys all called for more!

"Kneel down, then, and say the rosary first!"

Well, the boys didn't mind that. John led the beads and they all answered. And when they finished the rosary, John did many more tricks.

The news of John's skill spread very fast.

Then, one day, a lad who was several years older than John, and who was a very good athlete, dared John to race with him. All of Bosco's friends stood waiting to hear what John would say. After all, this was a big fellow!

"Yes, I'll race you: right now!"

And what do you think? John beat him!

"I bet you can't jump across that creek," said the athlete. He was hoping to win back his reputation.

The boys all yelled for their hero.

"Take him up on it, Johnny!"

"Yes, I'll take your bet," said John as he walked toward the stream.

The boys all hurried for places where they would be able to see the contest. They all wanted John Bosco to win.

Not far from the opposite shore was a low stone wall. The athlete hoped to jump far enough to be able to reach it. And he did!

Then John ran and jumped with all his might. Not only did he reach the wall, but continued over it!

From that day on, John Bosco became the leader of the boys in the village. He formed many clubs, taught the boys games. And their religion, too!

But as he grew older, John became more and more convinced that God was calling him to be a priest. And the thought made him happy.

John's mother was happy, too. But John's older brother, Anthony, was not at all happy about it. When he saw young Bosco with his head in a book studying, his brother complained bitterly to their mother about it.

Make John do some of the work around here, Mother. I'm getting tired having to do everything. He's always got his nose in a book. I'll fix him and his books!"

With that the older brother picked up the books and threw them into the fire.

"Don't worry, Mother. I'll get more books!"

"And don't you worry, my son. I am sending you to school in Castelnuova. You may have to work on the side, for we have little money."

And John studied hard! And he worked. First, he was a baker; then a tailor. Then, one day, a carpenter and iron-worker hired him. This man made beautiful things, and he was careful to teach John all he could learn.

When John was about twenty years old, he had a wonderful dream. He saw a beautiful lady standing in the midst of a flock of sheep so large that he could see nothing else.

"John," said the lady, "I want you to care for all of my sheep."

"How can I all by myself?" John exclaimed.

"I will help you!"

When John awoke he felt sure that the beautiful lady who had appeared to him in his sleep was the Blessed Virgin. He knew, too, that the sheep meant all of God's children. He was very happy. Nothing pleased him more than to work with children.

John now knew that the only thing for him to do was to enter a seminary and prepare for the priesthood. He was old enough, and he had a very good start in his education.

Yes, John went to the seminary. He loved the long black cassock he wore, for it kept reminding him of his great vocation.

But even in the seminary John did not neglect the boys in the neighborhood. He got them to play games; he showed them many of his tricks, and then he would teach them their catechism and some new prayers.

John worked hard at his studies. He knew how important they were. And because he was so busy the days seemed to fly by. Before long he had finished his course in the seminary. He was ordained on June 5, 1841. The happiest person present on that great day was his good old mother. More than once she had nearly died, but God was good to both of them.

Not long after his ordination, Father Bosco (In Italy priests are called Don instead of Father), found a boy in the sacristy one morning.

"What is your name, my friend?"

"Bartholomew Garelli. I don't have any home, and my people are all dead. Must I get out?"

"No, indeed. You stay right here. I need a friend like you."

It was a long time since Bartholomew had heard anyone call him a friend.

"Do you know any prayers, my boy?" asked gentle Don Bosco.

"No, I've never been to school."

Don Bosco then taught the lad how to make the sign of the Cross.

"Say, if I bring the gang around here next Sunday, will you teach us more things?"

"You bet I will. I'll be looking for you!"

And Bartholomew brought his gang. A dozen young lads. And each Sunday the number grew. Soon the building Don Bosco had rented would not hold all of the boys. Besides, neighbors complained of the noise they made.

"Well, fellows, next Sunday we will have to meet in the open fields outside of town. There will be plenty of room there, I'm sure!"

But Don Bosco still wanted a building, one large enough for a chapel and some workrooms. Finally, an old building was found. All of the boys helped to clean and fix it up. When it was all in order, things began to hum.

"Beginning tomorrow night, regular classes will be taught in printing, carpentering, tailoring, and shoe repairing," Don Bosco told his boys.

Soon other priests joined Don Bosco, and more such night schools were opened. Bad men soon began to think the priest had money, and they attacked him on a dark night as he was going home.

Suddenly, from nowhere, a big gray dog sprang at the throats of the bandits. One man fell to the ground and the others shouted to Don Bosco to call off the dog.

Always, after that, whenever Don Bosco was in danger, the great dog appeared at his side.

Soon some of the older boys wanted to join Don Bosco. Some he sent to a seminary to study for the priesthood. Priests, too, joined and were trained for their work.

In 1858 Don Bosco visited our Holy Father, Pope Pius IX, to explain his work.

The pope was very happy and gave his approval to the new Community Don Bosco started. It was to be known as the Salesian Society, named after St. Francis de Sales. After this many priests, seminarians and Brothers joined Don Bosco in his great work with boys. Later, he started a Community of Sisters to do like work among the girls. And both groups grew very fast.

Before long it became very clear to all that Don Bosco was working miracles. One day a group of 700 boys went on an outing with him. He promised them chestnuts when they returned from a long hike. When the basket was brought it contained enough for about 20 boys. But Don Bosco kept giving them out in big handfulls until the last boy got his. And there were some left over!

One day a poor mother brought her little crippled boy to Don Bosco. The lad had to use crutches to walk. The good priest's heart ached at the sight of the child.

"I bless you, Tommy, in the Name of Mary, Help of Christians. Now walk!"

Yes, Tommy was entirely cured. He threw away his crutches and ran to his mother!

As soon as Don Bosco had members of his Community prepared, he opened more houses, not only in Italy, but in other countries as well. And more and more requests came in.

But some of his priests began to worry about him. They saw how he was aging. They noticed the lines in his face, and that he walked much slower. Finally, they spoke to him about his work.

"We are very worried about you, Don Bosco. If you continue to work so hard you will ruin your health. Won't you please slow up?"

"Don't worry about me, Father. There is so much to do, and so little time."

"You are already past seventy. If you take it a bit easier you will be able to direct us for several years yet. We need you!"

But Don Bosco was not ready to give up yet. Many still came to him for advice. Many of the boys wanted to go to confession to him.

Later in the January of 1888 word spread that Don Bosco was dying. All of the boys in the school insisted on going to his room to see him for the last time. All prayed constantly that God would spare their good Father and friend.

On the night of January 31, 1888, while many of his Community knelt beside his bed, Don Bosco blessed all of 'his boys' in the Name of Mary, Help of Christians, and told them he would be waiting for them in heaven. Then he blessed all of the members of his Communities.

A few moments later, he closed his tired eyes and calmly died.

Miracles soon began to happen, and people from all over the world began to beg for Don Bosco's canonization. A very complete study of his life and writings was made by the Church.

Finally, on Easter Sunday in 1934, Pope Pius XI declared Don Bosco a Saint and set January 31 as his feast day. Since he loved children so much, ask him to pray for you!